Sound H

WILL EAVES was born in Bath in 1
novels, *The Oversight* (2001), *Nothing*
Paradise (2012, forthcoming), all publi_
poems, *Small Hours*, appeared in 2006. *Sound Houses* is his first full
collection. For many years he was the Arts Editor of *The Times Literary
Supplement*. He now teaches at the University of Warwick.

First collections from Carcanet Press

Caroline Bird, *Looking Through Letterboxes*
Linda Chase, *The Wedding Spy*
Peter Davidson, *The Palace of Oblivion*
Gerrie Fellows, *Window for a Small Blue Child*
David Herd, *Mandelson! Mandelson! A Memoir*
Katharine Kilalea, *One Eye'd Leigh*
Carola Luther, *Walking the Animals*
Gerry McGrath, *A to B*
Patrick McGuinness, *The Canals of Mars*
Kei Miller, *There Is an Anger That Moves*
David Morley, *Scientific Papers*
Togara Muzanenhamo, *The Spirit Brides*
Ian Pindar, *Emporium*
Richard Price, *Lucky Day*
John Redmond, *Thumb's Width*
Arto Vaun, *Capillarity*
Matthew Welton, *The Book of Matthew*
Jane Yeh, *Marabou*

WILL EAVES

Sound Houses

CARCANET

First published in Great Britain in 2011 by
Carcanet Press Limited
Alliance House
Cross Street
Manchester M2 7AQ

A CIP catalogue record for this book is available from the British Library

ISBN 978 1 84777 112 4

The publisher acknowledges financial assistance from Arts Council England

Supported by
ARTS COUNCIL
ENGLAND

Typeset by XL Publishing Services, Tiverton
Printed and bound in England by SRP Ltd, Exeter

To my parents

'The fact is that everybody has to stand the same racket, more or less.'

George Bernard Shaw, *Advice to a Young Critic*

Acknowledgements

Some of these poems were first published in *The New Yorker*, *The Times Literary Supplement*, *The London Magazine*, *PN Review*, *Yale Review*, *Other Poetry*, *Areté*, *The Age* (Melbourne), *Staple*, *Stand*, *Oxford Magazine*, *Poetry Review*, *Verse*, *Australian Book Review*, *Unknown Public Creative Music Quarterly*; 'The Field' and 'Roman Road' were included in *Best Australian Poems 2008* and *2010* (Black Inc.); 'Charity' and 'From Weymouth' were written for the band Spirit of Play; 'Home', 'Kickabout' and 'A Difficult Birth' first appeared in a chapbook, *Small Hours*, published in 2006 by Brockwell Press; 'Crater' was commissioned by *Tate Etc*; 'Bird Song', 'Silverflash' and 'A Year Later' were first broadcast on BBC Radio 3's *The Verb*.

Contents

I

Evening Lesson   11
Small Hours   12
Demonstration Day   13
English   14
Majesty of Nature   15
From Weymouth   16
Bloody Ill   17
Evacuees   18
A Kilburn Massage   19
Kickabout   20
Salomon's Offertory   21
Three Flies   22
Summit   23
Accommodation for Owls   24
Spider   25
Charity   26
Skimpole Abroad   27
Ariel in Texas   28

II

Hornets   31
Chestnuts   32
Gold Coast   33
Roman Road   34
The Former Resident   35
The Grass on the Other Side   36
Curve   37
Grounds   38
Crater   39
100,000,000 AD   40
A Difficult Birth   41
Cracked Happiness   43
Any Impediment   45
Bird Song   46
Kin Limbo   47
The Fight in the Lake   48

Horus and Janus   49
Clifftops, Folkestone   50

III

Avocado   53
Punk Revolution   54
The Field   55
The Clock   56
Elegies Around Noon   57
Footsore   58
Fantastic Blue   59
Home   60
Silverflash   61
Powers of the Minor Gods   62
Aberdyfi   63
A Year Later   64

I

Evening Lesson

Filling the slant, suburban lawn
A cybernaut with ducts for arms
Ponders before the sun goes down
If it will ever come to life.

The afternoon departed's been
Immoderately hot, the pets'
Tails curled like clefs, reptilian
On a bituminous pavement.

A kid, playing, knows for a fact
However long he waits he won't
Surprise the robot in the act
Of scooping up the puddled cat

Because the proof of what things are
When we're too busy not looking's
Obviously non-ocular.
His hands trip over rising scales.

He makes a sound the instrument
Alone cannot, and everything
In this setting is strangely lent
Purpose by dappled accident:

The chance note of definite shade
Beneath a Monkey Puzzle's knots,
The cat full-stretch and music spread
Across stillness to make it stop.

Small Hours

Temperature, night.
An air current, the
bunting they drag
across the forecast,
hides in an oak.

Up and down the street
a spectral army gathers
taking a leaf count.
Late cyclists skitter
through phantom ranks.

The sky is blown away.
I feel comforted.
Minutely lost to me
in the small hours,
your smile breaks.

Demonstration Day

Fifteen and short, I strode the cobbles
of Carnaby Street in August '83, and bought
a lemon-yellow tie there to the tune of 'ABC',
music no longer of its time but new to me,
as was the sleazy caff where I had lunch
(a peanut-butter, cheese and celery sandwich)
before tea and a doze, posing in Green Park,
stretched out like I came there every day to be
one of the crowd and nobody's fool. Really.
The hours inched by. I thought they'd fly

if I raced through the shops and galleries until,
hobbled by growing pains, blinded by genius art,
begged by a battery of nuns not to proliferate,
I escalated Underground and out of sight. But
I thought wrong: you cannot walk away from it,
refine the wait, hear bones stretch, set, say why
to lemon-yellow youth the style is not original. I
surfaced somewhere on the Northern Line with trees
and spent the weekend there. The details I forget,
like who spoke first, or first realised we'd met.

English

Ramadan means fewer taxis in the rain
so I run to the old Custard Factory
where no one knows how I knew you
and I explain in tribute that I hardly did:
for two years you read *Persuasion* aloud,
became my vision of JA: gat-toothed,
ironical, smiling encouragement
as I tried hard to get your tone (wise,
bottle-blonde, *au fait*) in my essays;
to make your careless insights mine
in double homage to the teacher
and the book I loved.

JA asked other boys, 'Who shot JR?',
and I was jealous when you laughed
at Ian Shrubsole's batsman's Cleopatra,
six beefy feet of Nile kine – no match
for my remarkably pitched Antony.
The century passed. Now, I'm a man
– in Birmingham, disguised by age
and facial hair, my speech ad-libbed
for once, yet still recalling how it felt,
those few unopened afternoons ago,
to hear in someone else's voice
the promise of my own, the fast
about to be broken.

> *O, I am trying, Egypt.*

Majesty of Nature

'At least a third of biomass
in any given area is ant',
our genial host explained,
his smile dog-fought by flies,
the long haul of a plane above
his head serenely interposed
between the insect and the void.

You see how they get started,
these creation myths: the seen is
not the point, apparently. You
have to take a closer look,
behind the gums swaying
like cheerleaders, to ants,
to life's original constituents.

High in the forest canopy,
a crow dies laughing at this
unevolved belief: that no one is
merely an entomologist, guide
or priest, but something much
more serious, albeit in glasses,
tidy piles and – *gotcha!* – pieces.

From Weymouth

What made you wake me so early
And with a look of mischief say,
A start this fine's surely a sign
The sea is calling us today?
The train was blue, the water green:
A tinted postcard sent in May.

I'm sure I must have held your hand
In backstreets crammed with grockle shops
And pubs and reeling fishermen.
The smell I couldn't place was hops.
I rode in state along the beach,
Beside the ride that never stops.

I missed a few easy lessons.
The teacher smiled, as if to say
It's fine – it would have been a crime
To hear the call and disobey.
What did you do? The train was blue.
We had tea at a beach café

And well-thumbed fish-paste sandwiches –
That gritty complement to hours
Spent toeing desperately the line
Around two limpet-clad towers
The sea and I besieged, the moat
I'm sure I must have said was ours.

What made me want to go early
And with a look of mischief say,
But I'm hungry? You wrote in haste:
His Highness made the donkeys bray.
The train was blue, the water green.
Yours, waiting by the beach café.

Bloody Ill

Flu-ridden for two days now,
I'm glad of the carpet; like Atlas,
a shoulder to lean on. Behind me,
the kitchen garners its grot:

ash, oatflakes under the lino,
lamb string, unstuffed stuffing,
grounds swilling the sink, floor
ripe with fridge roux. I miss it.

The plants will need water, too.
The spiders have blurted sprigs;
conkers, like swollen knuckles,
must be tended. I heard a split.

When my head thaws through
I'll sway at the stove's lip,
buy fresh and undivided milk,
dance on the crashed carpet.

Evacuees

Neither unmoved nor madly bereft,
suspicious of this crowded severance
from home, they stare perplexed – an army,
neat, drilled separately, then set
inside a carton of brass goadings
(Please Do Not Look Out) to glimpse
what grieving mothers look like. Only

one boy, invisible behind his
glassy breath, is stiller than the rest.
His nail, jammed in an easy grain
along the window's wooden rim,
chases arrow flight trails of summer
storms. He's eager to be gone, to wipe
these weathered faces from the pane.

A Kilburn Massage

Next door's lost three small vertebrae
so when her brain is starved of blood
her mouth opens and smashing sounds
come out. Tonight, it's crockery:
deep porcelain notes of Old English
reproach. I'm out cold on the floor.
The masseuse finds a tense muscle
and slams my back like a drawer full
of plates. One ear mashed to the ground
I catch the Tube's arterial refrain:
to hell and back, it says, with us
and our decorous bone.

Kickabout

I stopped sleeping and was afraid
that everything I did conveyed
the wrong message. A fat baldy allayed

my worst fears by ignoring them almost
completely. AFC Wimbledon, his club, could boast
Joe S., who once sat on the bench for Chelsea's first

team in the mid-'90s; and Darren D., reputedly
a mortician, who fired us three times past the post to deathless glory
in the Seagrave Haulage Counties League. We

went to every match, Baldy and me, our 57
obese with yellows and blues, him in his Saturday heaven,
me stupidly amazed to find that half of Raynes Park is Korean.

And it was therapeutic, I suppose,
to be a part-time bloke in borrowed clothes,
jeering the visitors from Basingstoke, cheering on those

especially who found an open goal and hoofed it wide.
I never wore the Dons' full kit, the colours. They implied
natural devotion, something unconsidered, more than pride:

comrades in arms, perhaps. Even the scarf I bought instead
felt too conspicuous. When I turned up, Baldy went red.
'I didn't recognise you like that', he said.

Across Kingsmeadow's terraces a gale of tact
exposed the true self muffled when 'opposites attract',
my effort to be what another hadn't known he lacked

until he saw the lack forgiven by buffeted eyes.
We won the cup. We split up, to no one's surprise.
The house of sleep is full of spies.

Salomon's Offertory

We have also men of radicall ingenuitie to build the
instruments of sound in different places, which by
extension and division of pipes in many sites and
combinations may represent the music of the very stone
cloist'ring their several constructions. We build one house,
and, as it were, one other within it so that the two, in space
and time, supply a mutual echo of the great machine (for
what else should we name the undiscovered sky?) above.
Also we interpret these sounds and structures as
exhalations by arts organic and mechanical. For of these
two principles are both houses naturally made; and if the
engines which build and inspire their frames are but raw
machines to proclaim *vox humana et angelica*, we have of
them also a breathing space which beyond valve and chest
endureth. And this we praise for an organic whole in
which the forme of all buildings and machines prevails
over their numbered parts. Likewise the architecture of our
sound has no fixed origin, being preserved by art of
substitution and repair that we may abjure the
preposterous wisdoms of authenticitie and all such vanitie.
We owe also unto these divers inventors that harmonies of
sounds both great and deep may be contained in small
spaces, like unto lives and memories that are within the
compass of a brain. And though we praise these harmonies
not for a true voice: insomuch as their huge warbling
in a dainty case may seem to mock the sacred echo of a
monumental house, but yet we are curious and seek a
means to mix and tame them. For what infernal place and
organ of distempered uproar could be more sweet, but
what we have not yet in our sound houses? And this
quiet fury of discoverie call we Pandaemonium.

Three Flies

Three flies on a rock,
Orion's belt in negative,
a cold beer in my hand.
And, after the storm, the day's
hot handkerchief shakes out
a flock of butcher birds,
black holes for eyes, from
Sugarloaf and Mount Buggery.
Calicivirus thrived up here
and didn't stop at rabbits.
Cane toads shipped in to eat beetles
ate everything else instead.
That's pest control for you!
I smiled. Which maybe shows
I like a poisoned chalice – the
creek, the hut, the iced-bun
reek of sunblock and repellant.
Butchers wait in the trees all night.
The stars settle. It's pleasant.

Summit

We climbed a nameless hill
to confirm the line of retreat.
Already the displaced inhabitants
were drifting back, their second youth
announced upon the scrolls of ferns,
sword grass, truncated trees.

Fire is the greenest torturer,
his schemes so wildly plotted
they come cacklingly undone,
the rocks broadcast like seeds,
the shaven ranks along the ridge
sprigging sedition openly.

The guns, wherever they might be,
have stopped, low mists implied
and, lolling in the early morning's
flashback blue, continued to deny
that anything had happened
as far as we could see.

The guest houses have shut for the winter.
The last bus out of here (and there are only two a day)
has gone. It's after five. And my new friends, Colin and Joy,
whose offer of a camp bed in an outhouse I've accepted gratefully,
are telling me about their courtship in the games room
of a mental hospital near Leith. *Axe-murderers*.

If I don't mind. Feel comfortable with the idea.
They fumble for a joke and go quiet.
We're sitting in a troglodyte's café-cum-shop
hewn from the rock – 'like Beethoven' – where
you can buy bacon and cream and bleached postcards
of green skies mantling Ben More, Mull.

The owner, moleish, fretful, spills sugar on the floor.
Aloud he says, though not to us, 'it can't be helped'
as if self-consciously remembering. Out in the bay,
his wife is winkling, spreading her salt-cured toes,
counting the grains that stick between
while others are dragged away.

Spare us your sympathy, Joy cries,
when over dinner I suggest 'it must have been awful'.
It was. A wilderness of frantic calm and Pictionary.
Nothing to read except Jumbo Puzzlers filled in and then crossed out.
Telly, of course. No radio. 'The things you missed were books.'
We walk down to the shore, clocked by Dervaig society:

a seal-like metronome
and high above the eagle's slow, unwinding beat.
Back at their stone-by-stone built house, Colin puts on *Kreuzer*
while Joy consults her concordance to Amerindian astrology.
I am an Owl with elements of the Goose. She yawns – it's almost one.
('Opinionated character. Night bird. Somewhat headstrong.')

Spider

The decoration moves.
It has eight delicate spokes,
discreetly hinged, that open,
close, lift, touch, retract
in a picky ritual of exploration,
unannounced, meekly insistent
that this green-girdered promontory,
like the other towers and half-built bridges
thrust at disappointing right-angles
to each other, should go somewhere,
have an end, meet more than air.

Her world today, this time, a room.
She has the species' knack for making
out the limits of a territory.
Great plains, sheer drops,
a flat vertical glacier
beckon on the year's far side
if her gift of patience provides.
Alone she waits in her perfect design,
soundlessly clicking into place
between two sticky monuments of spruce
an article of faith.

Charity

Look at the posters in plastic frames,
Shirts boil-washed to fit a pygmy,
Ties from a school that was recently
Closed and turned into apartments.
All of a crime's precious evidence,
Here in the warm room of no claims.

Behind the till sits a codebreaker.
She was a young girl at Bletchley.
'Certain things stay in the memory
Whether or not they're important,
Often because they're not important,'
She says. 'It doesn't much matter.'

Look at the collars with real names,
Books, games, a stainless-steel trophy
Lifted, discarded, then bought by me
Knowing I wasn't the first or best
And that envy can be laid to rest,
Here in the warm room of no claims.

Skimpole Abroad

Harold is in the swimming pool
shouting and creating a disturbance.
He's hauled out of the water, gasping,
and I discover he's a dwarf or a child.
I set him down and wait for him to grow.
When next I look he's turned into a tub
of gazpacho with a head on top. His own,

thankfully. Cut to a black car being driven
to a mental hospital in Northern Russia
which is where Harold has ended up.
We get out of the car and I ask for a few
moments to myself before we go inside.
I think we all know what we'll find.
Harold has landed on his feet again.

He's 'in the pink', according to the docs,
of whom my put-upon father, innumerate
and monoglot, is oddly one. Dad's fading.
He's ferried Harold everywhere all his life
– and now his life has gone. The ice thieves.
In every tongue Harold's a biding evergreen.
We die, but he, the holly king, is 'hanging on'.

Oh, drain the swimming pool! And stuff
A pillow in his chortling mouth! His need's
The gloating of a sun-plumped innocent.
And all his tenderness the sweet self-praise
Of one who calculated, giving to be given.
Harold flounders, protests his love for me,
For you. For the *borscht* in our veins.

Ariel in Texas

A devil, an eddy, an air ambulance:
I wish I were any of these things
and not the sort to raze where I have been.
Last night? Where was I last night?
Turning the bridge into a whisked piano,
making killer passes at cattle. The limit.

What would I not give to put things back,
spin blindfolds out of thunderheads.
No one, then, would look on my lowing
except as necessary grief, the wind
in wrangled spars astride the Brazos
and the buzz of telegraph wires.

II

Hornets

A few found the hole in the attic door,
crawled through and spiralled down the stairs
to meet my parents and an espadrille,

droning like mopeds, labouring uphill
into a thunderclap; wasps fed on electricity
to make them ripe and fat. This was at night. Disturbed,

in dreams I coughed up licorice and lemon curd
with feet and wings. Nippers picked at my mozzie net.
The generator outhouse buzzed allegiances.

By day we scoured Apt's rocky eminences
for souvenirs of sand: tan, ochre, red.
We were tourists, but didn't know we were

unless *le médecin avec un suppositoire*,
the fall-out from a feast of grapes, reminded us.
Or I got stung. I'd hung around the squadron's garret,

opened the door and briefly glimpsed the size of it,
their floor-to-ceiling unexploded bomb. The truth
spread hives across my skin. They'd made

us stay, be taken in. They'd called the fire brigade,
the medieval-looking special ops with gauntlets, greaves
and *poudre toxique* who breached the tower,

found nothing but sent us packing. That was power,
magic even, the way their strategy of evacuation
and coolly-regulated suicide missions

put the real nest beyond suspicion:
an outhouse in the gently humming trees
among small birds and, somewhere, bees.

Chestnuts

Why, this year, are they so flat, and many,
littering the bus stop's anarchised terrain,
on dimpled concrete and the preformed roof,
lodged in the grooves of seats that aren't
quite seats, on which nobody wants to sit?
The parent-tree echoes our clenched passivity,
standing in line, unable to assist its squirrel–
scorned offspring onto friendlier ground,
into the lowliest tract. They lie around,
resigned to their hard road, occasionally
picked up, carried a yard or so then dropped.
One cups a grain of plexiglass in its brown mitt,
oysterishly curved to meet the unforeseen
purpose, as if cut out to do just that.

Gold Coast

Back home the haughty word
event conjures horses, vowel-
swallowing, warbling tannoys
and money in a tent. Here

it means rain, the turnabout
of luck too slippery to be
stepped on; the first drops tea-
ceremonious, their cowbell-

clink of spoon in cup fat
with promise. After the shy
daughter, the Prodigal follows:
his stories loud, increasingly

dark, violent but apt, funny
as lizards filling up the rock;
and then the animals, people, tin
roofs drink in the shock of his

return, such high aqueous
humour! It is the perfect, boring,
flailing drum solo you never want
to end. The dowry. Downpayment.

Roman Road

A proud infant who will not cry,
the air stuffed full of *it's not fair,*
rumours of flood elsewhere in Poplar,
Plumstead, Lewisham. Not here,

though one dribbled blade slashes
the side mirror, its dots excitable as men
I once saw tracking gold on the Fosse Way.
Gluttons for drought, they lacked society

to give their store of interests ease,
dabbled with circuits, AC/DC, failed
almost universally. Maybe they found
what they were looking for in God

who isn't there and never was and so
cannot be lost. A few spots more, more
and still more. The strident pylons hum
approvingly, *fall in, hail Caesar!*

The Former Resident

'It was only when an arm-
adillo hit the window that I
noticed it, my house, gone,

and me, still inside. Someone
hooked it in the middle
of the night, drove us outta

town. I never heard a thing
till it flew past, staring
at me like I was crazy, like

I was the one in trouble.
Tell the truth, I wasn't sorry
to leave Mobile. I saw it more

as an act of God: my house
was took, but at least I,
I was took with it.'

The Grass on the Other Side

The Great White in the windscreen
Cruising at depths of 37K
Cannot conceive of being airborne
Or know that it is watched by prey
To whom life's second nature, as in
'I'm more myself on holiday.'

Another man who jumped the shark
When he felt he was dying now lives
And works in an Australian park,
At least he says he does. His relatives
Demur. 'It's all just talk, the infarct
Speaking, the impression he gives

Of happiness in another place.
Perhaps now that it's out of reach
His former self will recrudesce
And bring him back from Bronte Beach
To London where big fish are scarce
And schools, usually, the kids you teach.'

And maybe not. What do *they* know?
The suspect's vanished from the screen.
His mother burnt, his face aglow,
The freed man can't imagine
When and where he ought to go
Or what it is he should have been.

The sonar-beep of the bellbird
Implies no submarine except the one
That pointedly sounds bird-like, lured
To a perfect wattle-fringed lagoon
By other predators disguised
As families in the garden.

Curve

Around the hill the footpath bends,
Crosses the summit, then descends
Tracing our footsteps in reverse.
The wind is definitely worse
And you are quieter than before:
The mute expression of a Law

That says I'm not just tired and wet
But exponentially desperate.
I know this is the right way back;
The five-bar gate, the single track,
Those curtains drawn against the storm –
That could be us. We could be warm,

Watching a Bond movie ('Oh, James!')
And millions go up in flames.
Instead, the road begins to turn.
You disappear. I've yet to learn
That this is why it never ends.
Around the hill the footpath bends.

Grounds

Taller yews and smaller runs of box,
unguarded rose and poppy, threads of speedwell,
clumps of bluebell and forget-me-nots;

the path of old apples leading to grey lilac
past screens of cedars, firs enfolding still-forgotten
Christmases; cow parsley, dandelion, stock.

Crater

Too much success can ruin you,
I've heard it said. Look at my face.
Look at the full-blown moon's gasp
Of astonishment, her lidless ecstasy
The blind side of renown, the silent
Shelving of attention after the race
Is over and the tribute won.

Her own rites had long cooled
When my flame lit under the sea
And Neptune warmed to my ascent.
It took ages. I've watched all kinds
Swim, paddle, flutter, fly, become
No one's idea of 'what was meant
To be'. An idea meant for no one.

Friend, I'm not even here. Or if I am
I'm just your voice in a closed room,
Clamouring against torrential dark
Poured out on a hot moonless night.
That isn't the home crowd roaring.
It is the rocket ship, the sound
Of visitors who came and went.

Vulcan has left the building.
Some took self-portrait snaps, flashes
Of scalded time. Others kicked stones,
Looked at survival's great endeavour
And, unimpressed by dust, turned
Round to find a world behind them,
Glowing, dawning, radiantly lost.

100,000,000 AD

The Captain's keen to explore, go deeper,
Take core samples, measure astronomical tilt.
He says the clues are down there with the truth;
Our forebears, numerously well-preserved,
Point to the paradox of their success: death
Learned from them and wore a cunning face.

We throng the younger layers of sediment,
Lie curled in the embrace of great forests
That overran new land, perished, grew back.
And lower down we're much in evidence, too,
Across the globe, a race undrowned and diligent.
We were much smaller then. We cowered and hid.

The mystery is in the interval, the Captain says,
Where nothing but the same poor pollen remains.
No larger predators, no cat-like cometary snarl,
Only a grin composed of mystery's missing teeth.
The Captain works so hard he barely eats his kids.
What happened, what happened?, he squeaks.

A Difficult Birth

In his 'Napoleonic Wars',
The banks of Borodino thronged
With italics, *swiss rolls of flesh and blood*
Packed tight against pike-staff margins.
The book, a hundred pages leaded
By the heavy glint of 7B, horses
Deranged and men and Death
Rampant, flowed red.

He bought it in a shop on holiday
In France, wrote every day and didn't wash.
Our blow-up tent hummed with the hornet-thick
Disgrace of clever kids who just get cleverer
And clean forget to stop. He drew far better
Than Dad, deaf even then, for whom talent
Was not enough, who smacked him
Right across the gob.

We shared. He smoked at night
And blew the smoke into a cigar box,
The trove of heroes: warriors, crooners,
Weirdos mistily remote, splendid in fields
And rings and screaming halls. The Hurricane.
The King. The Greatest. Lord Carnarvon,
As he signed himself in Wales. To get
A rise, he said, a look.

One time in bed, our loyal adjutant
(The Carpenter) radioed above a seashell roar:
'He's won the title back at thirty-two – *What*
An incredible man!' I still flinch at the scent
Of that sweat-soaked and all-redeeming victory,
Its trace-echo of fags and joy on my own words,
Their filched and processed, unembattled
Volume of delight.

And now he squats in Hastings,
Packing meat, the foreman to a force
Of wreck-toothed immigrants. His latest god
Is Shackleton. I could so easily be him, see him
Becoming me, transient among the bus shelters,
The wankers' brie. For this is how it always
Ends when bad luck throttles you at the start.
You fight, instinctively.

Cracked Happiness

a birthday poem for Fiona Gruber, with facts from
The Scholar's Book of Useful Information

1

A labour of moles in Australia
is fast of Greenwich by ten hours,
their total saleable output not given
(unknown) in metric tonnes.

'One of Mark's many greatnesses
is his ability to persist
in doing something long after it's
been proved pointless', *id est,*

he puts moles firmly in the shade
with his extremes of industry,
harvesting *marrons de Lyon*
under pinpoint immensities

no one can really hope to grasp
without a powerful telescope
(and even then it's quite a stretch
to find credible witnesses).

Consider the End. Or rather, don't.
Look past the tree into the way,
milky with morse, the sky encodes
our sceptic's fear of fruitfulness.

2

From the colour-mixer's point of view,
a most delicate primary: yellow
requires the greatest care,
as yellow sullies easily.

Looked for, the mood alters.
There's no sufficient quantity,
no pinch of guilt, will make it fair.
Because the taste of beer batter

and seagulls' tottering gluttony
on a deserted shore belong here, Fiona,
it follows that they belong nowhere else.
And when the tender cypresses renew

their felt-tipped hue, resist the lure
of much greener comparisons. Courage
attend your nosediving barometers
after so many years of drought, thunder

and lightning play on the Rialto.
P.S. Your husband's home. Slight structural damage
may occur. If not, the dog will certainly oblige.
de dah de dah de [end of message]

There are no moles in Australia.

Any Impediment

My love, there is a problem with the rats.
They're stuck together like chicken breasts.

If it were merely mingled tails and claws
I wouldn't mind, but some of them will

need a knife. What if the portions tear?
I do not want to see their bodies split

along a plane of tender grey weakness,
lest with the leakage and the residue

I should become appallingly familiar.
Upstairs your son's helical pet flickers,

catching the scent of strange deference,
the great taboo of what we find ourselves

doing mostly because we are afraid not to.
Forgive me, love. But I can't marry you.

Bird Song

The unfamiliar bird will come
when no one in particular
is looking out or feeling low;
when nothing much needs to be said
      or can be done,
that's when the bird will come.

He wasn't there a while ago
to make this song familiar
in ways no one could have foreseen,
ways that conspired to remind me
      I didn't know
myself a while ago.

If I leave now perhaps he'll stay,
the unfamiliar visitor,
and take the next chorus alone.
He is the strangest of strange birds
      I've met all day.
Assuming that he'll stay

I ought to make my excuses
and while he's singing disappear,
as if there's nothing to be said
or done about the way I feel
      used and useless,
the fit he induces.

And suddenly the bird has gone
along with his particular
fear of the too familiar;
because I whispered in his ear,
      'I know this song',
that's why the bird has gone.

Kin Limbo

Between Christmas and New Year comes respite
when we retire, with whispered thanks, to berths of solitary joy
and find ourselves closer, concealing rifts and making memory
right; the daily tasks – cleaning, answering cards, grouting
the sink – fulfilled in convalescent mode; work worries,
ambition, the knotted string of tense relationships
unpicked and set aside for the time being.

In such a mood, spontaneous trips to see
the Mummers of Marshfield bred family tradition,
an uninspected Boxing Day ritual, peripheral, valued:
St George, half-cut, a plasterer arrayed in paper rags
like windblown lath, slayed his dragon (the magistrate)
every half-hour from war memorial to pub and back.
A truce called on imaginary slights, the trivial past,

over mulled wine and scavenged carcasses.
More recently, our pantomime convoy
to the deer park in grating frost fell easily apart,
like a train of thought. And you and I, the outer
siblings, happy to be adrift (or so it's said), steered
not-so-happy inner, older ones back into port.
Mother, mother's brother, inseparable,

who mewed feebly if we walked off, watched us
like sullen children when our eyes rolled on the heath.
Two polystyrene cups of tea from a collapsed, roadside trailer
restored order, reminded me of Marshfield and the cold dumbshow;
how people with a martyr's studied history learn one version
and stick to it, shocked by the suddenness of their own hate
should young stirrers demur. 'You've got a vicious streak!'

'You're so selfish!' Rightly superior in their suffering
(tenements, bombs) and sad. Why did we have to be so different?
What's wrong? They watch their gift to us, our greedy flight bluewards,
unleashed, turn threatening; their lives eclipsed, made dragonish.
War forged a sword of gratitude on which they, thankless, fell.
I use some soap to smooth white silicone around my sink
and float in kin limbo. And draw a kind of blank.

The Fight in the Lake

Unseen, unseeing when first I breathed this element,
I had some blood-inkling of what would come. I heard
the tabor by the treeless lake in my dam's heartbeat
and the monster's gargling of birth sorrow,
her cries for Grendel, butchered son.

Her shriek was mine.
I knew it from afar, the curdled yell,
deep issue of the mountain's wintry melt and thrashing mother-slime.
Some wordless vengeance brings me low as once I thrust into the world,
head bowed, hands curled, the mite born furiously aware of balances:
I grasp the rock-scoured, icy pans of keep and waste.

Fear stirs the silt. The miry depths grow grappling fronds,
the snake-coils hide Hrunting. Like silver roads at dusk, the sword's
light fails.
It will not lift, though by its last gleam I see something rise
out of that wrack to which the fiery angel fell, a half-quenched shape.
By Hrunting's faded charm I glimpse the she-shadow, her yellow eye,
the gaze gated by teeth and hate and son-remnant, closing.

Into the treeless lake-mirror I passed and slew, with my bare hands,
the thing I saw.
Scorning the sword I reached for flesh and wild hair.
I pressed my thumbs into a neck of strings and tore their music out.
The wafted gore entered my mouth. I taste it still as she is hauled from
her foulness.

Blood-inkling quickens. She curses air.

The eagle peals: *harden your heart.*
Upon the rocks I dash her gouting head. Her froth of agony resolves
into a rill of words: *run far from me, your own despair, slobber and run*
as an infant mourns a soft voice turned to stone on which his tears rain down,
in vain run to the drum of dismayed pride, O Geat, to the harrowing sea.

Horus and Janus

The Stars

As streetlights flick on like a dead bulb coming back to life,
the trip-switch *tink* of extinction becomes a bright keynote.
Its timbre has no echo, not really, unless that potted lemon tree
by the door, bit to the root at birth, a dogged stump that strengthens
every year with calm neglect, is rattling sympathetically. Could be.
Beside it lies fruit-shaped, plum-like and leaking on the underside,
a not-yet-rotten windfall. *Destiny bakes it in a load of cobblers.*

You did the washing up! Twice! And my ears unblocked,
aptly enough, while I was plastering a crack over the sink.
Emblems of domesticity, these are the miniscule repairs
to tiles on vessels entering an atmosphere of resistance,
the torrid marriage of air and delicate gesture, the tact
of good advice withheld, that spare us unexpectedly.
The hardest wax eventually migrates outwards, I hear.

It's true the seasons are melding. I see the summer clouds
exploding silently and know it's wrong. *Destiny runs for
a bus.* That lemon tree, the vast harvest, the strange fruit
and a plague of vicious parakeets that don't belong anywhere
near. What can I do but lose myself in dead-bulb stocktaking,
counting the times I have not counted accurately the times,
the countless ways that something happened surprisingly?

Personal History

My horoscope is adamant: I have 'the power
To change even a stubborn mind'. I'm not so sure;
Had I the power, would it be mine to self-conquer?
Accept changes to one damn thing after another?

Clifftops, Folkestone

The smoky further light makes Dungeness
Power Station battery-sized.
Nearer, a rifted sky lets fall Perspex
while nearest, right in front of me,

the crows of the New Metropole court dance –
black dressing for the red-brick squares
of chimneys schooled in five
sombrely useless pairs.

A gull raised high on its bent weathervane
conducts the chorus of the calling flock
who seem interested but do not know how to sustain
a note, don't care (are *birds*), and past their audience

of bemused hotel visitors and vague front desk,
the jazzed-up ranks of one more spent era,
towards the Channel's endless groove
slide and career.

III

Who would have thought my shrivel'd heart
Could have recover'd greennesse? It was gone
    Quite underground; as flowers depart
To see their mother-root, when they have blown;
        Where they together
        All the hard weather,
Dead to the world, keep house unknown.

George Herbert, from 'The Flower'

Avocado

Whenever I see its shady canoe
I think of cleft lightbulbs, of you
who had your first at fifty and thereafter
occasionally ordered half as a starter,
as a reward for unspecified privations –
thin clothes, rationing and operations.
The kick of it and not the taste
was what counted. Your wits erased

by mockery, you joined in with a prophecy:
'I'm only allowed one thought a day.'
But your one thought, your half a notion
of 'riotous living', escaped our attention.
Now when I buy a crib of three,
I wonder at their cut-price luxury,
the cost of carving that last canoe
in which your son abandoned you.

Punk Revolution

She sat facing us, back to the telly,
   as we looked over her shoulder,
      laughing, and she laughed too

because we were funny that way
   when we, her children, were laughing,
      happy, and she was happy too.

She couldn't see the band gurning,
   the faces that were pulled behind her,
      though some part of her wanted to –

because she was funny that way
   when she heard young voices calling,
      angry, and she was angry too.

I sit facing her, back to the present,
   as she looks over my shoulder,
      smiling, and I smile too

because she is funny, that way,
   when she, my mother, is smiling,
      happy, and I am happy too.

The Field

Each room's a hillside of thorn,
Its objects colouring under a look;
And everywhere the scatterings of life,
The gimcrack stools and cabinets,
The foxy dark beneath a bed,
The regiments of books unread
And put-away blankets flower
Because beheld. This evening
Thistles open. Not looking back,
A neighbour's ruffian son cries off,
Sent home for playing William Tell
On his front teeth at a Big Do.
Come eight o'clock the light
Across the road and Harry Belafonte's
Yellow Bird between them butter the street.
Singing: around and up the stairs we go
To hand-me-down bathwater, views
Of the town spread like a jewelled beast,
Griefs towelled to bits, their wounds
Prickling over, oblivion, clover.

The Clock

She inclines to the case
Where a few pattering syllables
Suggest a carillon under the heavy flow,
A peal reduced to ash-clogged monody
  In the bell tower.

It came from Cuiyusuru in Mexico,
The badlands or Eden in retrospect
After the hurling hill and cannonade,
The glowing locust harvest,
  Covered its maker.

El señor de los milagros!
His work rescued in blind panic
By careful hands. We lost the letter of provenance.
Handless and cracked it tuts, she clucks, a duel
  Of blanks on the hour.

Elegies Around Noon

1

I wish I could have sat with you more often,
downstairs, when you came in from the garden
and your afterlife of raising flowers
instead of kids: late roses, broom, hibiscus,
latterly a fig. The bramble by the steps
fruited for weeks, suckering closer
while I grew hopeful twigs, poked stones,
rolled words like 'forest' round my mind,
then heard you shout from the kitchen:
Christmas. Christ. Not again. I'd stained
the pastry red but everything was soon all right
and I was free to go back out while you stayed in.

2

You told us you'd been trapped in the pasture,
behind a strip of salt marsh and sea gorse,
by cows, advancing silent condemnation
of your drystone perch and deft picture.

'You have created a scandal
with your lunchtime desertion, Cecily,
leaving the herd to their ice cream-fuelled raillery;
to stubbed toes, sunburn, hit-the-can and tears, as usual.

They will miss you. They just don't know it yet.'
And frightened by such brown, eloquent eyes
in which the tide was high but turning,
you scrapped your drawing, and left.

Footsore

The room is warm.
The lady's turned every two hours.
A drying pot.

The train has been delayed
but absolutely will come
in a moment.

The signal's up and go.
Beyond the laurels, playtime.
And beyond that a single-note

lament, high, pure,
refined by shock: Doris.
Her toenails being cut.

I'll have you. I don't want it. Oh!
The room is close, the train closer.
Green talons yield their stubborn crop.

Fantastic Blue

You could be very funny, too.
    On that last canted stagger through
The care workers' housing estate
    Towards Peasedown St John High Street
And pizza you would never eat
    Cooked by a Turkish Cypriot
We got to know during the week,
    Your panicked, wandering husband took
You past wasteland and tore a head
    Of buddleia from its brick bed.
And with 'Hey, Ces! Fantastic blue!'
    Stirred some deep instinct to be true;
Not to endorse decades of error
    By going even one step further:
You stopped. 'It isn't blue, 's purple.'
    First utterance in days of drivel
And unintelligible whisper,
    Garden to upstart gardener.
Your guide considered ruefully
    The evening's hue of accuracy,
Liver and rage and aubergine,
    The hanging baskets of Peasedown,
Not knowing what if anything
    He'd ever meant to her – meaning
His wife, not this shaded creature –
    And picked another.

Home

Birds wake to a daily loss of care
And sing the measure of the dawn,
The reddening width of your eyelid,
The world while I was being born.

It is the hour of disarray
That catches you alone in bed,
A prey to all the visitors
Who come and go inside your head

Until a woman's voice downstairs
Topples the crates of memory.
The clattered light behind a blind
Is like responsibility.

Lie quietly. Be unafraid.
We come upon the world undressed
With each rising – it doesn't mind
And this is not another test.

Silverflash

Not since I was four or five at most
and in the first of many striped tee-shirts
have I been this close to the flavour of safety.
I'm walking into town again, the child of hills.
You bought me fish and chips for lunch, my own
adult portion because I asked for it, in Evans's
tiled restaurant, the Alhambra of takeaways.
Fine living robs the faculties of right judgement;
I turned, lost sight of you that afternoon in M&S.
Gone, and the unworn self at once puts on habits
of wandering. ('Have you seen my ...?')
They stood me on a counter. You appeared
and recognition bore away the riderless hoofbeats
of fear. Pride claimed me, later, when you praised
my instinct to be visible, which soon became
the need to be noticed – a confused stage,
a knowingness that wasn't what you'd meant
at all! You were relieved to see I'd asked for help,
could be that lost and, knowing it, be found.
My deep-sea stripes helped you spot me,
their colours sliding past, today, in town,
the blue and brown and silverflash of cars
like keys to some fastness. High ground.

Powers of the Minor Gods

He knows – he *knows* the men who drive the grey three-wheeler van
kidnap young'uns like me, not him. I do not want to run.
I want to fall through winter woods, down flights of pie-crust steps
broken by roots, past lone lamps and their spidery circles

out into Prospect View: a high dog-walk for kinder souls
who have no cause to talk yet whistle cheerfully, follow
a lead because it's late. The valley glows with pinpoint gold
while it grows cold – and I'm not even halfway home or safe,

electrically alert, wired to stay alive, a yell
ahead of bundling thieves whose hands clutch at the gears of fate,
the non-slip wheel, the *Mercury*'s small ads for help with debts
incurred, places to rent – on, on, along the wind-blocked path

to the main road that I must never cross. But I'm possessed.
And those with gloves and string approach. For dear life I empty
myself ... the door opens. You ford a pounding headlit stream,
one finger to your lips, which I ignore. Once we're ashore,

it all comes out. I had to leave my friend and not look back.
I'd glimpsed a hungry cage, heard bad laughter; thought of this house,
spin dryer, gas fire and deaf, chair-bound spinster neighbours at ease
with every shake and fold of the retold adventure. So

what happened to my knowledgeable friend? We pass on fears
we cannot contemplate. The sceptical inspire belief.
You called to make sure he'd turned up, in case. Was he the leaf
I took from someone else's book in order to escape?

Aberdyfi

It's a gentle kind of pain
Like a dried-out river plain;
What has flowed won't flow again.
Though they sometimes sound the same
Echoes in the sub-terrain
Repeat to fade another's name,
   And of that I've no right to complain.

Bells ring out under the main
Like a slowly spreading stain.
What went wrong? I can't explain.
When a stranger calls your name
It's a different source of pain,
Though to me it feels the same.
   Yes, I know I've no right to complain.

Being honest, being plain
Takes away one kind of strain
But its absence is more pain.
On every frequency the same
Distress signal whispers in vain:
Change the subject, change the name,
   Neither one of us can then complain.

A Year Later

Since you went back underground,
Into a world of solid waiting rooms,
Drip-fed arches and choked retreats,
You've been airily visible, present,
Returned, a burst seedcase and slow-
Growing regret: the morning light
Condensed where you once stood,
The dusky loss its own dividend.

Your sockets ogle worms' contrails
Crawling across the firmament, so
Near to voices you suspect of life
In a familiar house on a drained hill.
(To cloistered shades, sense-memory
Must tantalise the way the senses did.
What is this substitution for feeling?
Why can't I see the trampled sky?)

It needn't be that strange. You are
A dream – the self unself-aware –
And when a likeness raises you
(My rooky laugh, the waft of tea
Carried outside) we're not surprised
Though I have learnt to be discreet
And lower my eyes. To be recalled
You do not have to prove yourself.

Now all those duties become ours.
Your time of worry has given birth.
When most you're missed, I seem
To see a rope thrown ship to shore.
It has to flee the outstretched hand
And carve new purpose in the air.
Often the searching gaze conceals
The very thing it's looking for.